A KILLER SHARK

TOM JACKSON

WAYLAND

First published in 2011 by Wayland

Wayland
338 Euston Road
London NW1 3BH

Wayland Australia
Level 17/207 Kent Street
Sydney NSW 2000

Editor: Julia Adams
Designer: Paul Cherrill for Basement68
Picture researcher: Tom Jackson

Jackson, Tom.
  A killer shark. -- (Animal instincts)
  1. Sharks--Behavior--Juvenile literature
  2. Sharks-- Life cycles--Juvenile literature.
  I. Title II. Series
  597.3-dc22

ISBN 978 0 7502 6586 7

The author and publisher would like to thank
the following agencies for allowing these pictures
to be reproduced:
All images and graphic elements: Shutterstock, apart
from: pp. 4–5: Dreamstime; pp. 8–9: Dreamstime; p. 9:
Jeff Rotman/Getty; p. 10: Brandon Cole/Photolibrary;
pp. 10–11: Stephen Frink/Science Faction/Corbis;
pp. 12–13: Dreamstime; p. 13 (top): Dennis Kunkel
Microscopy, Inc./Visuals Unlimited/Corbis; p. 13
(bottom): Jeff Rotman/naturepl.com; p. 17: Dorling
Kindersley/Getty; pp. 18–19, 31: Steve Bloom Images/
Alamy; p. 19 (inset, tuna shoal): Dreamstime; p. 19
(inset, sea lion): iStock; p. 21: Visual&Written SL/Alamy;
p. 22: iStock; pp. 22–23: Suzi Eszterhas/Getty; p. 23: Jeff
Rotman/Photolibrary; pp. 24–25: Jeff Rotman/Corbis;
p. 25 (inset, top left): Mark Conlin/Alamy; p. 25 (inset,
top right): AFP/Getty; p. 27 (top): iStock; p. 27 (bottom):
Doug Perrine/naturepl.com; p. 28 (inset): Jeff Rotman/
Alamy; pp. 28–29: Santiago Armas/Xinhua Press/
Corbis; p. 30: iStock.

Should there be any inadvertent omission, please apply
to the publisher for rectification.

Printed in China

Wayland is a division of Hachette Children's Books,
an Hachette UK company.
www.hachette.co.uk

 CONTENTS

Giant hunter — 4

All at sea — 6

What's that noise? — 8

The whiff of blood — 10

Built to swim — 12

Feeling for prey — 14

Friend or foe? — 16

Attack! — 18

In the jaws — 20

Predator or prey? — 22

Meeting humans — 24

Finding a mate — 26

Saving sharks — 28

Quiz — 30

Glossary — 31

Index — 32

Giant hunter

Great white sharks are the world's largest hunting fish. These **predators** are big enough to fill a football goalmouth and they weigh more than an entire football team put together!

Dorsal fin

Eye

Pointed snout

Mouth

Gills (used for breathing)

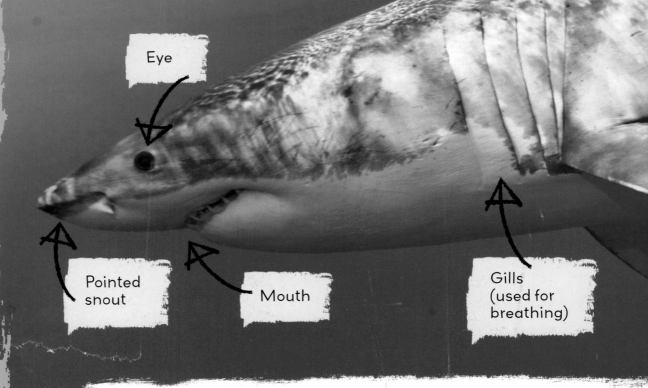

Monster cousin

Great whites are not the biggest sharks of all. The whale shark is twice the size, but it is also harmless. It eats plankton – tiny plants and animals that float in the sea.

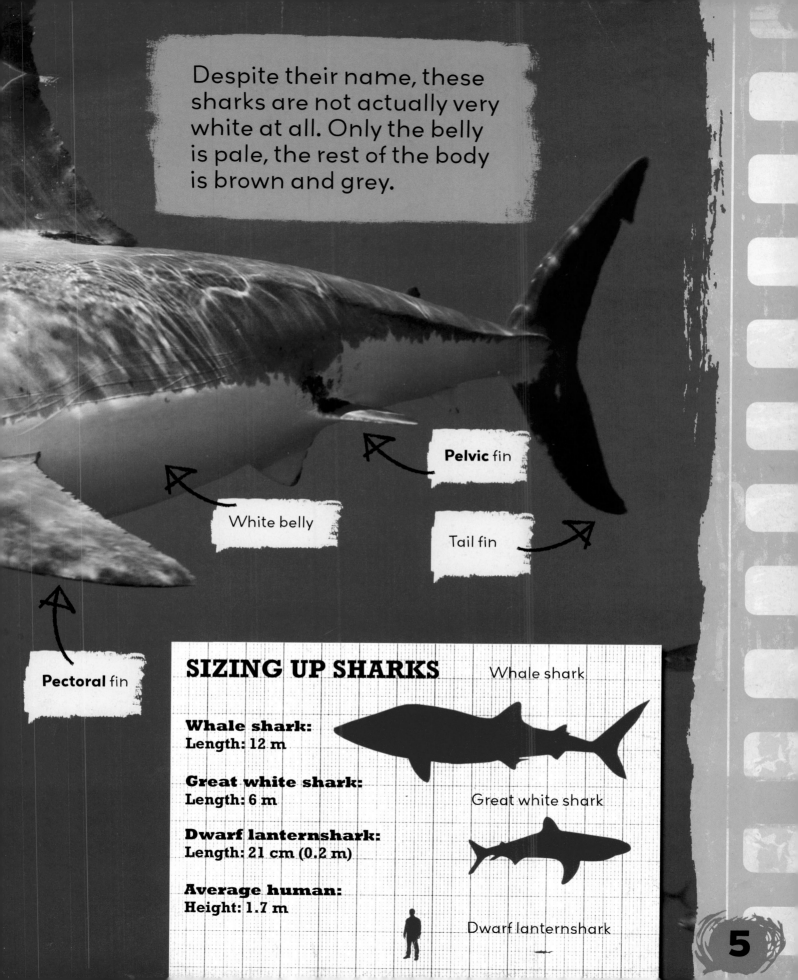

Despite their name, these sharks are not actually very white at all. Only the belly is pale, the rest of the body is brown and grey.

Pelvic fin

White belly

Tail fin

Pectoral fin

SIZING UP SHARKS

Whale shark

Whale shark:
Length: 12 m

Great white shark:
Length: 6 m

Great white shark

Dwarf lanternshark:
Length: 21 cm (0.2 m)

Average human:
Height: 1.7 m

Dwarf lanternshark

All at sea

Great whites do not hatch from eggs, like most fish. They are born, like humans. Experts think that the largest pup eats its smaller brothers and sisters inside its mother before being born.

All I have ever known is the wide open sea. I have been living alone since I was born. I stayed out of the way of bigger sharks when I was small. Now I'm big, most things stay away from me!

Great whites start hunting after birth. They become adults at the age of 15.

I make long **migrations** each year. In the summer I visit islands and coasts where there is plenty of food.

Great white sharks live in parts of the ocean that are cold. They use the heat coming from their huge muscles to warm their body.

WOW!

A great white pup takes 11 months to grow inside its mother. That's two months longer than a human baby.

what's that noise?

A great white shark is always on the look out for a meal. The first clue it gets is usually a sound that it picks up with its sensitive ears.

Did you hear that? It's only faint but something is making a splash. It's probably a fish struggling to swim. That would make an easy meal for me, so I'm going to take a look.

A shark's ear is just a small hole in the side of its head

WOW!

A shark can hear a fish splashing 250 metres away. Human ears can only hear it from about 70 metres.

Sea birds dive for sardines, because they live just below the surface of the water. Sardines are too small for a shark, but a shark will sometimes try to snap up a bird!

IN THE KNOW

Fisherman in the South Pacific use sounds to hunt sharks. They rattle shells underwater to fake the sounds of splashing fish. Any sharks that come to investigate are killed with a spear.

The whiff of blood

Sharks have a very strong **sense** of smell. They are especially good at sniffing out the tiniest amounts of blood in water. A shark could smell a teaspoon of blood in a swimming pool.

Sharks search for blood because bleeding animals, such as this ray, cannot swim well enough to escape an attack. This means they make an easy meal for the shark.

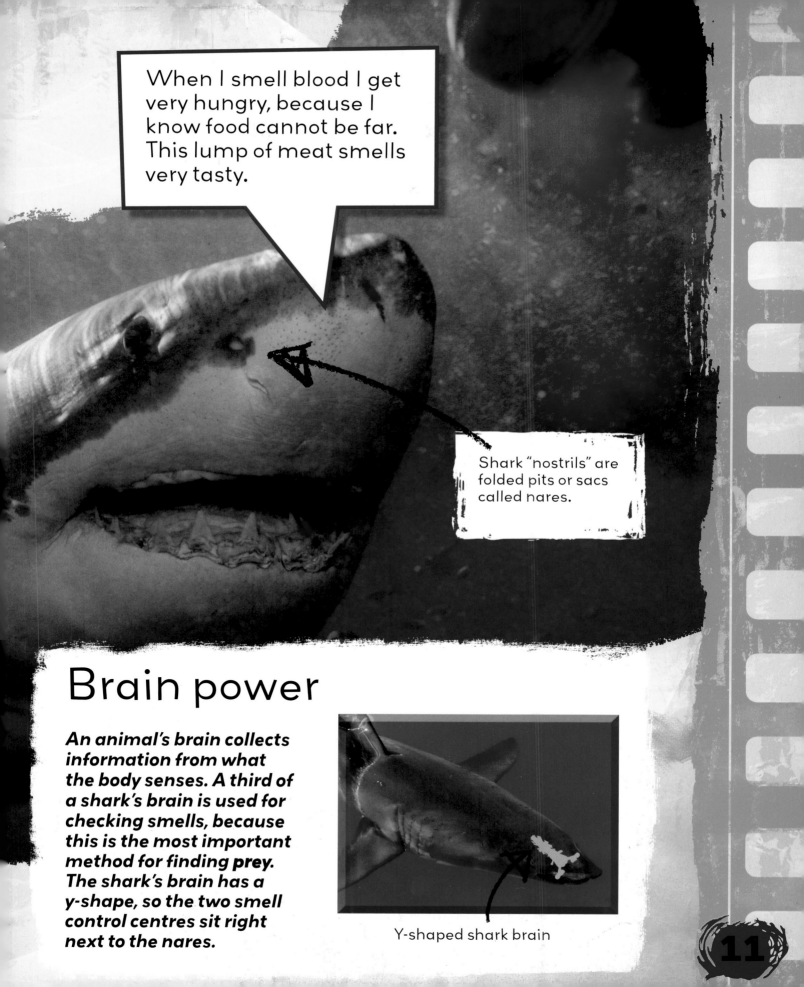

When I smell blood I get very hungry, because I know food cannot be far. This lump of meat smells very tasty.

Shark "nostrils" are folded pits or sacs called nares.

Brain power

An animal's brain collects information from what the body senses. A third of a shark's brain is used for checking smells, because this is the most important method for finding prey. The shark's brain has a y-shape, so the two smell control centres sit right next to the nares.

Y-shaped shark brain

Built to swim

As a hunter, the shark is always on the move, trying to find prey. Its body is a swimming machine. It can keep going for days without getting tired or out of breath.

Swimming is easy for me. A swish of the tail is enough to push me along. I steer with my side fins. I rarely stop moving forward, otherwise I'd begin to sink.

Dorsal fin stops the shark from rolling on its side.

Gill slits

WOW!

A great white shark swims five times faster than a person can.

Side fins work like wings stopping the shark from sinking.

A shark's skin is covered in tiny sharp scales, called denticles. These make the skin as rough as sandpaper. They help the shark to slice through the water.

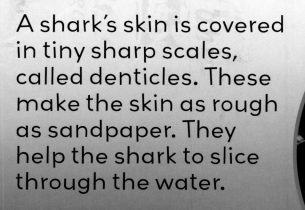

Denticles

Tail fin

Breathing in water

A shark does not breathe in or out like us. As it swims, water comes into its mouth and flows out through gill slits. On the way through, oxygen from the water passes into the shark's blood. This oxygen helps to power the body.

Gill slits

13

Feeling for prey

Sharks can only see what is in front of them and above them. So they have extra senses to help them pick up what else is around them. They can sense the tiny electrical currents that each living body gives off in the water.

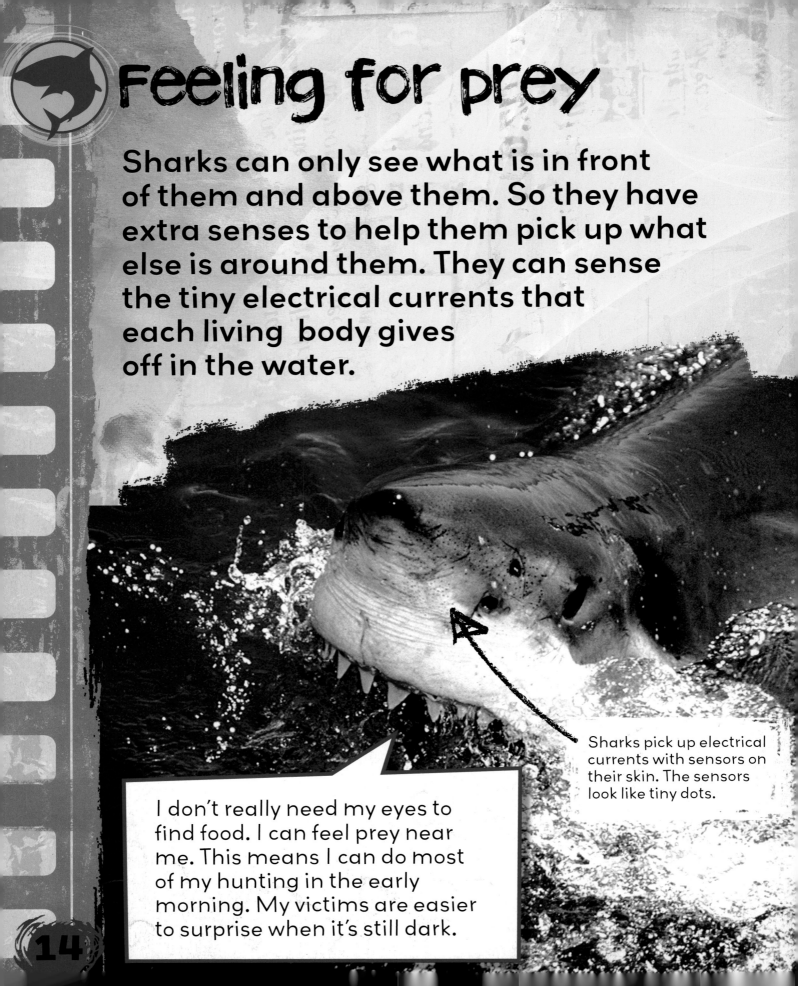

Sharks pick up electrical currents with sensors on their skin. The sensors look like tiny dots.

I don't really need my eyes to find food. I can feel prey near me. This means I can do most of my hunting in the early morning. My victims are easier to surprise when it's still dark.

When fish or other animals swim, they make little currents in the water. I can feel these currents on my skin. I always know when an animal is close by.

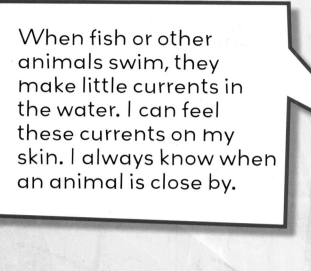

The great white shark's water current sensors run along the side of its body.

IN THE KNOW

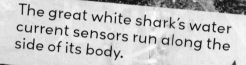

The great white shark's colours make it hard for prey to see it from above and below. From above, its dark top is a similar colour to the dark ocean. From below, its white belly blends in with the bright surface of the water.

friend or foe?

Sometimes, prey attracts more than one shark. Only one of them will be able to attack and eat the prey. But which one?

Another shark is hunting the same sea lion as me! I swim above him to compare our sizes. The bigger shark will have the first go at attacking.

Shark swimming past below.

Talking like a shark

When great white sharks meet, they check to see which one is the biggest. They do this in four stages:

1. They swim past each other to compare their length.
2. They have a look from the side to double check.
3. The bigger shark wins, and the smaller one always gets out of its way.
4. The smaller shark hunches its back to signal it has lost.

1.

2.

3.

4.

attack!

Great white sharks have a set way for attacking different prey. Large animals, such as dolphins – or people – are normally attacked from behind. A smaller victim, like a sea lion is hit from below.

Sometimes a shark's attack is so powerful, it jumps clear of the water.

I hit the sea lion hard. Now it should just take one bite. As I surge in for the kill, I roll my eyes back to protect them from damage. I can't actually see what I'm biting.

The small sea lion is knocked out by the first bite. It will be too badly injured to swim away.

Top Targets

Great white sharks are not fussy eaters. They will eat all of these animals if they catch them. Each animal has its own tactics to avoid being on the shark's menu:

Sea lions hide in seaweed forests.

Turtles use their shell as armour.

Tuna form large **shoals**.

Seabirds fly away when a shark attacks.

Whale calves stay close to their mum.

Dolphins fight back as a **pod**.

in the jaws

A great white shark's jaw is one of the deadliest pieces of killing equipment in nature. However, not all shark bites are meant to kill prey.

I like fatty food. I often nudge prey with my snout before attacking. If it wobbles enough, it will probably taste good. I'll then give it a small bite to check how it tastes. If it's all skin and bone, I'll swim away.

Sharks have two rows of teeth.

IN THE KNOW

Most people who escape from sharks do not escape at all. The shark lets them go because they aren't fatty enough. The shark doesn't like the way people taste.

A bite is normally enough to kill prey but I often have to wait for bigger victims to bleed to death. Shaking them from side to side speeds things up.

Shark teeth are razor-sharp and have **serrated** edges, like a saw.

WOW!

Sharks grow 3,000 teeth in a lifetime. Humans have just 42!

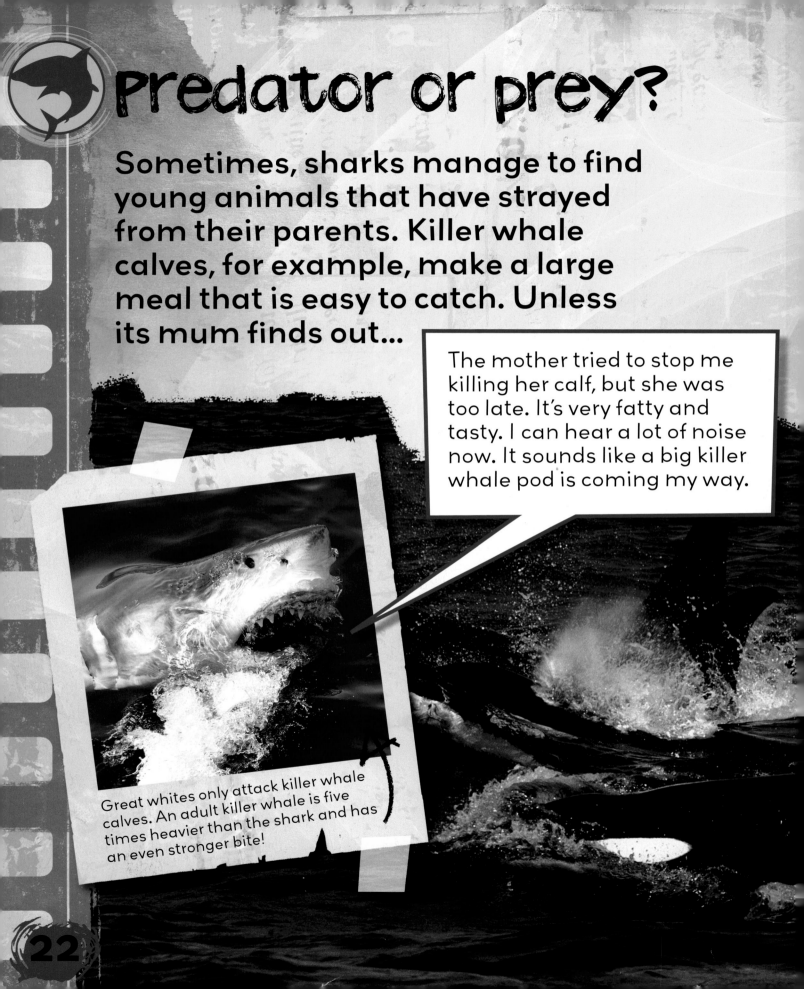

predator or prey?

Sometimes, sharks manage to find young animals that have strayed from their parents. Killer whale calves, for example, make a large meal that is easy to catch. Unless its mum finds out...

The mother tried to stop me killing her calf, but she was too late. It's very fatty and tasty. I can hear a lot of noise now. It sounds like a big killer whale pod is coming my way.

Great whites only attack killer whale calves. An adult killer whale is five times heavier than the shark and has an even stronger bite!

The whales are attacking me! They are trying to spin me on my back. They have almost managed. I've never really been turned upside down before. It's very confusing.

IN THE KNOW

When sharks are turned on their back, they fall into a trance. In this state, they cannot move and will drown. Some killer whale pods have found this out. They flip great whites on their back and eat their liver.

Killer whales try to flip sharks on their back. If the sharks don't get away, they could become prey themselves!

23

meeting humans

In order to study sharks, scientists sometimes go into the sea in metal cages. Then they attract the sharks with bloody chunks of meat, called bait.

There is a person here. The person is surrounded by something very strange. It is shiny and hard, but it also makes my snout tingle, a bit like a shoal of fish would.

The shark can sense electric currents coming from the metal cage and the diver.

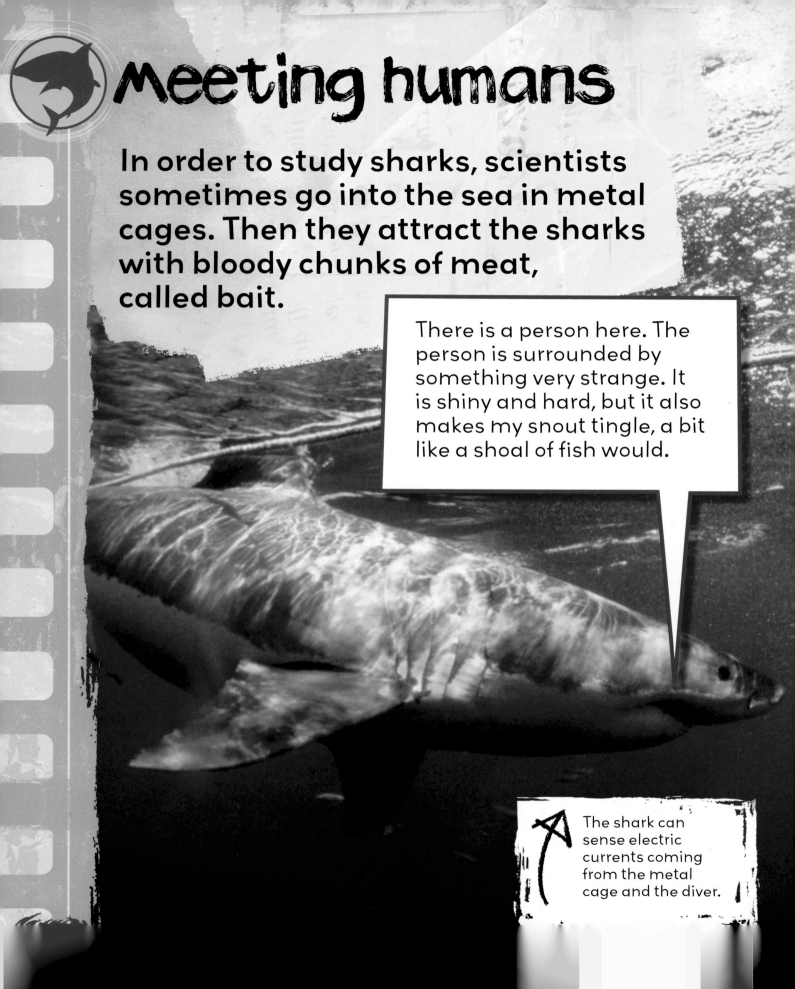

WOW!

Sharks can eat 200 kg of meat in one meal. That's about 400 times more than a person eats in one meal.

Scientists use long poles to attach a tag to a shark's fin.

Scientists attach tags to sharks. A tag collects information about where the shark goes. After three months, it falls off the shark and floats to the water surface. It then sends its recordings to the scientist.

Underwater camera

Sharks often bite the cages.

Finding a mate

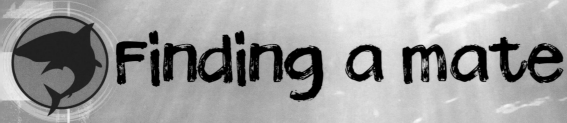

No person has ever seen a great white being born. We do not even know how the sharks find a mate. Shark tags may tell us more, but until then it remains a mystery.

I'm off to search for a mate. If I'm lucky, perhaps next year my pup will be swimming in these waters.

Some scientists think that sharks mate after they have had an especially large meal.

26

Shark eggs

Not all types of shark are born. Small sharks hatch out from eggs, sometimes called mermaid's purses. These eggs have squiggly tendrils which tangle with seaweed on the seabed. This is so that the eggs don't get washed away.

Tendrils

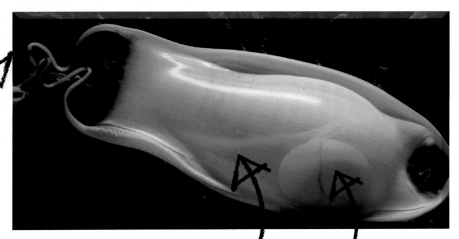

Baby shark growing inside an egg.

Yolk sac

Great whites and many other large sharks first develop in eggs, too. They hatch out of the eggs while they are still inside their mother. Then they grow more and feed on the fatty liquid from the egg's yolk sac.

Newly born lemon shark pup

Yolk sac

Mother

saving sharks

Great white sharks are very powerful animals, but they still need our help. No one knows how many great whites are swimming in the ocean. However, people kill so many sharks each year that some types could become **extinct**.

Sharks are often killed in nets. They can get trapped in fishing nets or nets that stop them from getting close to beaches. When they are trapped, they can't move and die.

A diver cutting a dead shark free. Sharks drown when they get caught in nets.

Sharks are caught for their meat. The fins are used to make soup.

Sharks kill about six humans each year, but humans kill millions of sharks in that time. Food and sport fishing kills 200,000 sharks every day.

It is against the law to fish for great white sharks. However, **poachers** do kill them and sell their body parts. Some people will pay a lot of money for the tooth or the fin of a great white.

Large great white shark teeth cost US$800.

QUIZ

1) Sharks have a very poor sense of smell. True or false?

2) How many teeth does a great white grow in its lifetime?

3) How many people are killed by sharks every year?

4) What would happen if a great white shark stopped swimming?

5) A shark's brain is shaped like a 'U'. True or false?

6) What do sharks breathe with, lungs or gills?

7) Where are a shark's electricity sensors?

Answers:
1) False. Sharks can smell blood from hundreds of metres away.
2) A great white grows about 3,000 teeth in its lifetime.
3) About six people are killed by sharks every year.
4) A shark would sink if it stopped swimming.
5) False. A shark's brain is Y-shaped.
6) A shark breathes with its gills.
7) The shark's electricity sensors are on its snout.

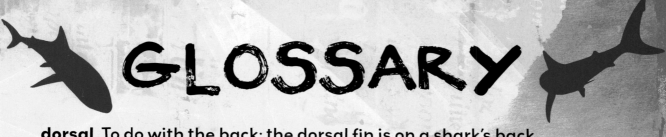

GLOSSARY

dorsal To do with the back; the dorsal fin is on a shark's back.

extinct When all of one type of animal, or species, dies out forever.

liver The largest organ inside the body.

migration When animals make long journeys to find food, mates or a better place to live. The journey is always a round trip because the animals eventually return to where they started.

oxygen A gas mixed into air and water that is used by a living thing to release energy from food to power the body.

pectoral To do with the chest area.

pelvic To do with the lower body area.

poacher A hunter who breaks the law by killing animals that are protected hunting bans.

pod A group of dolphins or whales.

predator An animal that hunts for other animals and then kills them for food; great whites are the world's biggest predatory shark.

prey Animals that are hunted and killed for food by predators.

scales Waterproof plates that cover a shark's body.

sense To hear, feel, see, taste or smell something.

serrated Something is serrated when it is covered in a zigzag of spikes and is used for cutting.

shoal A group of fish.

trance A relaxed state when the animal is awake but might behave like it is asleep.

Index

Blood 10–11
Brain 11

Denticles 13
Dolphin 18, 19
Dorsal fin 4, 13
Dwarf lanternshark 4

Egg 6, 27
Electrical currents 14, 24

Gills 5, 12, 13

Jaw 20–21

Killer whale 22, 23

Lemon shark 27

Mating 26–27
Migration 6

Nares 11

Pectoral fin 5
Pelvic fin 4
People 18, 24–25, 26, 28
Poachers 29
Predator 4, 22–23
Prey 11, 12, 14–15, 16, 18, 20, 21, 22–23
Pup 6, 7, 26, 27

Sardine 9
Scientists 24, 25, 26
Sea bird 9, 19
Sea lion 16, 18, 19
Sense of smell 10, 11
Sensors 14, 15

Teeth 20, 21, 29
Tuna 19
Turtle 19

Whale 19
Whale shark 4, 5

Animal Instincts

Contents of titles in the series

A Curious Dolphin
978 0 7502 6588 1

Clever dolphins
Born to swim
Taking the air
Wave riders
My gang
Sensing the world
Seeing with sound
A fishing trip
Snapping up food
Meeting humans
Taking a rest
Meeting a mate
Saving dolphins

A Fierce Lion
978 0 7502 6587 4

Mighty lions
Living with Mum
Joining the gang
Food for the pride
Meet the neighbours
Forced out
Sensors on
Hunting alone
Dinner time
Taking a rest
Ready to fight
King of the pride
Saving lions

A Deadly Cobra
978 0 7502 6589 8

Scary snakes
Hatching out
Silent hunter
My patch
Getting a taste
Death bite
A long, slow lunch
Danger approaches
Facing the enemy
Meeting humans
Captured and milked
New for old
Saving snakes

A Killer Shark
978 0 7502 6586 7

Giant hunter
All at sea
What's that noise?
The whiff of blood
Built to swim
Feeling for prey
Friend or foe?
Attack!
In the jaws
Predator or prey?
Meeting humans
Finding a mate
Saving sharks

WAYLAND